A Walk Down the Rift

The Poetry Pin Project

Published by

Fly Catcher Press

A Walk Down the Rift

Christopher Jelley

lead poet

Tracey Roberts

project co-ordinator

ARTlife

Davina Jelley

photography

Contents

9   Changes

13   Land Locked Literature

17   Spring   Elaine Necchi-Ghiri · Christopher Jelley · Steve Pledger
                          Tracey Roberts · John Scholes · Richard Westcott

37   Summer   Terry Gifford · Christopher Jelley · Davina Jelley
                          Richard Mackrory · Elaine Necchi-Ghiri · Harry Ward

63   Autumn   Christopher Jelley · Davina Jelley · Will Rayner
                          Tracey Roberts · Harry Ward

81   Winter   Geoffrey Bailey · Matt Bryden · Christopher Jelley · Davina Jelley
                          Helga Staddon · Lucy Summers

104   The Final Word

107   Walk the Rift

109   Acknowledgements

Changes

A Walk Down the Rift captures in words and images a story of change along a narrow strip of land dividing rural, coastal Somerset from a new nuclear power station building site.

In this incongruous landscape, dislocated and emotionally-charged, we invited poets to walk the trail to record the changes and to reflect on Year One of a massive ten year construction project.

As government agencies, local authorities, pressure groups and protesters monitor and challenge the impacts (positive and otherwise) of the development on the environment, on communities, on tourism, and on jobs and the economy, ARTlife's Poetry Pin project offered a way for people to express their personal thoughts and feelings within the complex debate around nuclear power generation.

Poetry is a powerful medium in which to explore our emotional connection to place and the landscapes we feel a part of. Two hundred years ago, Samuel Taylor Coleridge trod the same path as Poetry Pin down to Shurton Bars, a stunning geologically-rich coastline; and there he was inspired to write a love poem to his wife-to-be and to the spirit of the landscape that so captivated him – 'Lines Written at Shurton Bars' (1795).

His time in Somerset was the catalyst for the emergence of Literary Romanticism, a movement that opened people's eyes to valuing nature and natural beauty in its wild and untouched form. The heritage of Romanticism is the wealth of protected landscapes that we enjoy today as National Parks and Areas of Outstanding Natural Beauty.

The fields, hedgerows and drovers' roads around Hinkley Point A and B power stations, and the building site for C, are far from untouched by human hand. And yet the poems in this collection suggest a strong sense of shared connection to the land, of wanting to safeguard what has become beautiful with time and familiarity.

There are poems about fear of change, about loss, about anger and feeling powerless, about the bewildering implications of technological and scientific advancement, about being a small cog in an unimaginably large wheel. But there is also humour, wistfulness and a nod to our literary heritage.

For ARTlife and the Poetry Pin team, this project has been a high-wire walk, as we endeavoured to balance creative autonomy with an acknowledgement of the investment that made the work possible – impact mitigation funds paid by the power station developer to the local authorities in what is undoubtedly the biggest planning agreement this part of Somerset will see in a generation, and an investment of millions of pounds that has polarised local opinion. In the tension between opportunity, anxiety, apathy and acceptance, we have tried very hard not to fall to either side of a very high fence.

We hope you will enjoy this walk in the footsteps of poets and perhaps choose to visit the Poetry Pin trail and the ancient holloway down to Shurton Bars, adding your own thoughts to history in the making.

Tracey Roberts

Land Locked Literature

Close your eyes and imagine walking across freshly planted meadowland, the trail then drops into a clearing where you disturb deer that scatter beneath a murmuration of starlings. The hedge line encloses over you forming a natural tunnel before rolling up and down towards the sea, and all the while showing glimpses of a wire fence with acres of untouched grassland beyond.

This was the very first Poetry Pin workshop walk along the ancient holloway which connects the hamlet of Shurton to the Bristol Channel; the first of twelve months geolocating poetry along this three quarter mile stretch from March 2014. It was a year of inviting people to walk and write poetry to be digitally tethered to this trail in a way not possible just a few years before.

The concept of Poetry Pin is simple; add words to a pin on a digital map, to reveal on your mobile phone when in that same physical location, in this case Hinkley Point Somerset. It entitles both reader and writer to engage with space and locality in a brand new way.

A single tap on your mobile phone is all that's required and Poetry Pin is there in your hand guiding you to the poetic interventions along the trail. Flighty and ethereal, it is real but not real, like a spirit you can summon on a whim for your delight, a new invisible layer authored into the landscape.

Now with the year's workshop walks at an end, we have witnessed the beginnings of the build at Hinkley Point. We have traversed this place again and again, slowly fashioning little pockets of land-locked-literature ready to be divined through the wings of satellites.

These fizzing vortices of poetic engagement truly beg to be consumed in their natural habitat, out there along the trail. Seeded beneath the wide west country sky and exposed to sun wind and rain, they somehow become free.

I suppose it is because they are born from their location and dilute when dislocated from it, which in itself creates a peculiar dilemma whilst extracting them for this publication. Without their homes these poems become orphans, corralled and sanitized by the inking and formula of paper.

So reader, don't read on, put on your coat and get down to Shurton Bars, your couch can consume you another day, go taste the words pinned on the breeze by authors who trod that trail before you. The trail awaits, what shakes?

Christopher Jelley

spring

Spring

21	What Shakes?	Christopher Jelley
22	Manifested Irony	Steve Pledger
23	Beginnings	Tracey Roberts
25	The Green Corridor	Elaine Necchi-Ghiri
26	Greasing Palms	Christopher Jelley
29	Shurton Bar	John Scholes
31	Rights and Wrongs of Way	Richard Westcott
32	Jackets	Elaine Necchi-Ghiri
35	Kitchen Crumbs	Christopher Jelley

What Shakes?

Just bite it, and write it,
word it, then site it.
Park your mark to this path,
for the next to read on their digital pass.
The canvas awaits,
what shakes, what breaks?
A trail of traits,
all shapes and mistakes.
Only here can you gather the rhythm and flow,
the dips in the trail or the rain on your brow.
Untethered and exposed, released and refreshed,
word-smith extrusions, juices freshly pressed.
So, stitch it to the trail,
put a notch in the rail,
post it, haste it,
chain it, and paste it.
The canvas awaits,
what shakes, what shakes?
The canvas awaits, what shakes?

Manifested Irony

On land which has kept and sustained us;
By waters that ceaselessly roll;
We're asserting our claim to dominion
Over forces we cannot control.

Steve Pledger

Beginnings

Setting out

Poems poised

in a mind full of expectation

We tread the path of old and new

And the mud slides under us

As quietly

The land makes way for change

Tracey Roberts

The Green Corridor

A green corridor links this world to ours
Fox holes, trees and golden flowers
Chain link fence and warning signs
Keep Out. Keep Back. Trespass Not.
Stay Out. Stay Back. Forget This Spot.

Butterfly hovers, the air is fresh
The grass so soft, but the fence is mesh
Keep out. Keep back. Venture not.
Stay Out. Stay back. Forget this spot.

The tractor drones, the children play,
Some people walk along this way,
But once again, the same refrain.
Keep out. Keep back. Linger not.
Stay out. Stay back. Forget this spot.

Elaine Necchi-Ghiri

Greasing Palms

Back in the day before Benholes Farm
Back before EDF crossed Lady Gass' palm
Back before atoms were considered for smashing
Before errant school girls were punished by lashing
When the holloway was cobbled and paved
And the residents grew crops for local sea trade
Spelt and barley whose husks still remain
Our ancestors brewing and eating the same grain
Fragments sifted by modern trowel
And through this dust we frame their lives
Of locals who toiled beneath ancient skies
With broaches and boots adorning their dead
And corpses too with severed heads
Or legs removed from below the knee
As we lift them from their ancient beds

Pock-marked remains from diet so thin
We marvel at beakers placed within
The crook of the knees in the father's grave
By hands of brothers, sisters, sons
A line of genes which run and runs
Down to the hands of those who exhume
And collect their remains for cardboard tombs
Acid free boxes in warehouse stores
Filed and bagged amongst further scores
The relatives of ancestors who lived the same
Buried their loved ones with the same pains
Who lived on this earth and on spoils from the sea
And died right here on the land of the free

Now heavy plant erases this past
The ancient field lines their homes and hearths
The round house footings but resistive measures
Captured by technicians mapping these treasures
Are now removed for new history in the making
Shelve the past for its the future we're breaking
And all that's captured in this land
From ancient works to quern stone grinds
Turned and terraced
Rolled and topped
Dug and drained
Burnt and mocked
Mashed and sealed with heavy plant
All made possible with a government grant

Which perhaps could have all been nipped in the bud
In one subtle contract some time ago
If the honourable Lady had just said no
But the irony in these noble finds
Whose footprint stretches back across time
Without this costly intervention
Would not have disturbed our ancestors' slumber
Nor the bones of a further number
And with it the knowledge and lineage
Ancient lives and relatives
Those who toiled this land before
Tenacious hands running keel upon shore
Depicting a portrait of who we were
A blue print of who we are still
And our graves to come in these tidy hills

Christopher Jelley

Shurton Bar

At Hinkley Point did EDF
A stately power plant decree:
From whence, some iffy water ran
Through pipeline measureless to man
Out to the Bristol sea.

So twice five miles of fenced-off ground
With lights and cameras girdled round.
Beyond, lie meadows bright with sinuous rills,
Here blossoms a lonely lampshade-bearing tree;
And here are footpaths ancient as the hills,
Enfolding sunny spots of poetry.

John Scholes

Rights and Wrongs of Way

The Right of Way still wends its way
between these spiky hedges
here the shepherds drove their sheep
and goods came from the sea.

Straight alongside, strictly ruled
the new fence struts its sharpness
here you're noticed, watched and warned
Keep Out - the path has been diverted.

Beyond the field an aerial mobius
free-willed vortices of starlings
there an unheard murmuration startles
away over muddy old lane and clean steel fence.

Richard Westcott

Jackets

Red - the jackets of the six men fishing,
Preparing their bait in the sand.
Balanced along a steep rocky spine,
They stand with their rods in a line.

Yellow - the jacket of the old man paddling
Along the shore in the waves,
Cap on head, trousers to knee,
He stands with his dog in the sea.

Pink - the jacket of the young girl sitting
Serene and alone on a rock,
Wind on her cheek blows hair undone,
As she sits with her face to the sun.

Gone - the jackets of the children playing;
Jumping on rocks, all worries forgot.
With heads unadorned, no shoes on their feet,
They run to where sea and sand meet.

Elaine Necchi-Ghiri

HINKLEY RIGHTS OF WAY CLOSURES

WL 23/95
WL 23/95
WL 23/95
WL 23/95
WL 23/95
WL 23/95
WL 23/61
WL 23/48
WL 23/68
WL 23/70
WL 23/105
WL 23/70
WL 23/71
WL 23/43
WL 23/46
WL 23/56
WL 23/110
WL 23/110
WL 23/110
WL 23/110
WL 23/110
WL 23/56
WL 23/53
WL 23/45
WL 23/56
WL 23/69
WL 23/56
WL 23/64
WL 23/48
WL 23/60
WL 23/56
WL 23/57
WL 23/58
WL 23/56
WL 23/67

Stogursey
West Somerset
1 May 2012
P1-2012
P. Silvers
220001 - 14539
884

Definitive Footpath
Restricted Byway
Subject to closure
ROW Subject to closure
native Route

Kitchen Crumbs

Our legions ride with pens in their spines
and the track rolls and slides like ancient times
badger deer starlings boiling
kissing gate to the chain-link coiling

'Keep your hands off the fence don't touch the wire'
hollow smiles efficient attire
circling slow the compound trail
monkey got words monkey got tail

Past the bat house and the Tacky-shade collector
past the laminate maps part eaten by nature
down to the geo with the clints and the grikes
boulders smashing by little tykes
paddling free in the murky brine
beneath scoured stone Bars slumbers serpentine

All change all change as we scatter to scribe
scratching in the sand drawing words from this tide
over the wash and across the Bars it comes
and we mop up its moods like kitchen crumbs
caressing us fleeting we pen the words for keeping
Poetry Pin prose for posting and tweaking

Christopher Jelley

summer

Summer

40	A Walk Down the Rift	Christopher Jelley
42	Hinkley Point	Richard Mackrory
43	Empty Words Filled	Harry Ward
44	Waking Thoughts	Christopher Jelley
47	The Walker's Companion	Davina Jelley
49	The Building's Lament	Elaine Necchi-Ghiri
50	The Firm	Christopher Jelley
53	Dark Flecks	Christopher Jelley
54	Untitled	Harry Ward
54	Hinkley G	Terry Gifford
56	Pantiles	Richard Mackrory
58	Better Places	Christopher Jelley
61	Flippant Legacy	Davina Jelley

A Walk Down the Rift

The trail unfolds with fresh secrets stored
A depth of meadow now lush and bold
The heat of this day misses the beat
Slipped away lazily, a gracious defeat

A pace, a state
A place, a fate
Pursued by haze
Uncoupled, un-phased

And the 'C' sleeps in limbo state
Mounds of earth pushed like peas on a plate
We all await the maelstrom descent
An inertia of policy none can prevent

So we count the common blues
The cinnabar moths with their curly cues
The rills of the meadow rich and compact
Ironically provided by this industrial pact

The day is lost now grains through the slot
A joyful addition easily forgot
A fragment of time others dismissed
A shake in the timber a walk down the rift

Christopher Jelley

Hinkley Point

Eye catcher or blot on the landscape?

Clean, secure, affordable source of energy for five
million homes
Cancer cluster in Burnham
A way of tackling climate change
The only legacy will be a pile of nuclear waste
42% in favour
83% against
Part of a long term economic plan
A target for terrorism
A great day for our country
Chance of a catastrophic accident

Do you tell the truth or do you deceive?
Who exactly should I believe?

Richard Mackrory

Empty Words Filled

So we took a walk,
Reading poetry,
Increasing our inspiration,
And know-etry,
Surrounded by nature and all its grow-etry.
Our cultural carriage drawn by ideas,
Stopping only for lunch, the noble steed veers,
As the Sun from behind grey clouds peers,
The modern edifice spreads its nuclear fears,
In their hearts, the poets, shed peculiar tears.

Harry Ward

Waking Thoughts

In my nightmares I swim in the ponds
amidst the isotopes and their fiery blue legumes
or down in the heat of the boiler space
cooled suit all cosy on the reactor face
inspecting quadrants inside the machine
cave diver's gene but way more extreme
and down in the basement where the cooling ponds rest
one hundred days calming before the flask dispatch
and again in my nightmares I swim down there
amidst the isotopes in their fiery blue flare
with my sievert count beyond the blister
and the safety chants of procedure procedure

And still in my mind I swim down again
pearl diving freely with no mortal pain
and snatch at the pellets in their innocent glow
breathless amidst the boronated blue
nightmares come during my waking day
my thoughts compress this stuttered re-play
and again I sink in the boronated water
repeating and reliving my self suffocating slaughter
the bubbling of consciousness the fear of fear
shake the mood and memory clear
again and again I find myself drifting
into the poisons of memories shifting

Christopher Jelley

The Walker's Companion

I can sense the high sky
there is no need to look up.
Today my eye seeks pleasure in ruffled green,
pinpricked with innocent blue
and a ditzy of daisies.

Insistent they command my attention.
With Summer shrill
they tumble and skitter.
Dance upon naive feather.

In their joy they encompass that blue.
Cross my constant companion.
He who has not deviated from my side
as we amble to the sea.

Yet, when we reach the cliff edge
he does not leap down
eager to warm his spine against smooth rock.
He has promises of power to protect
and strides out East.

Davina Jelley

The Building's Lament

I look towards the Boundary Fence,
To a world that's new and exciting.
Where starlings dance and daisies grow
And deer run free through the
Warm sun's glow.

That place is beyond my Boundary Fence
And it's one that I cannot reach.
Still I watch and I wait, but the way
Is blocked, with the lock set fast
On the gate.

And through the Fence I see people walking
Free, with their heads in the sun.
But although I am here, in the light and the glare
There's no kindness, just fear, as they stand
And they stare.

I yearn to be free of this prison of hate
To work and to light and to heat.
But all I can do is stand and grow blue
As I listen for news
Of my fate.

Elaine Necchi-Ghiri

The Firm

Cut the ribbon
Prime the reactor
Pull the rods with the Chinese contractors
All smiles and shine to the chain reaction
Atomic construction policy distraction
Ramp it up till it's critical
Balancing parameters with the theoretical
Systems run and systems set
Black marks in history are hard to forget

So who'll be the first to charge their phone
Switch on the light Hoover the home
Who'll be the first to suck on this dial
Drink from the elixir of Frankenstein's vial

Who'll be the one who clocks up the bill
Plugs in their heater when the night turns to chill
Who'll despair when the future arrives
Energy poverty - pounds in their eyes
Sixteen billion to prime this machine
But the profits oh the profits are far from lean
And we need this, we need this
For the dying and the poor
For the little old lady with white wellies by the door
For the child born early in the plastic box
For the factories and museums and the charity shops

For the tired

For the cold

For the vulnerable

For the old

For the good

For the many

For the pious

(If there are any)

For the darkness

For the ride

For the slowly rising tide

For the frail

For the infirm

And for the directors of this firm

Christopher Jelley

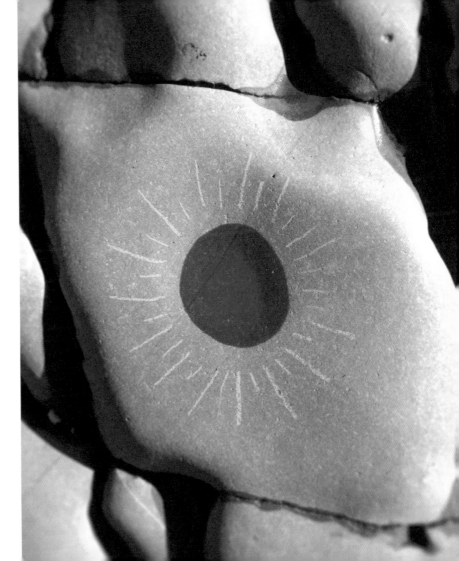

Dark Flecks

Rain blasts neat
sweeping through the vale
dancing on the grass tips
humming through the rails.

Rattling over coat hoods
and steeling over sands
dark flecks on pebble banks
smooth and warm in hand.

Silks of corn quivering
in this bowing chase
scavenging rills, and dancing drills
scatter in its grace.

Flexing life and trailing light
swift madness of this motion
authors scratch at their pads
tapping the commotion.

Patterns sketched patterns traced
heady frictions part displaced
back we crawl to our slumber care
and leave the corn all dancing there.

We've pocketed the memories
like badges on lapels
and slide back through the words once more
to capture vital spells.

The gravel crunch the holloway
the green tunnels the serpent's spray
the wire edge the steady lament
and all before the storm's descent.

Christopher Jelley

Untitled

Hinkley G

Power of the Sun,
Inside, Fenced off,
Access to none.

Blinding morning sunlight
on rippled sand still
running with rivulets
of star-pulled tide-drain
the old energy undated
as yet, to be decommissioned.

Harry Ward

Terry Gifford

Pantiles

This isn't Tunbridge Wells
No Georgian colonnades
No royal connections
Nobody taking the waters

They came from the Netherlands
Landed on Parrett shores
Exchanged for wool and cloth
Shipped along the waterways

Later made in Somerset
Unique in the west
The true Bridgwater tile
The flat-and-two-rolls

Tile ribs running down slopes
A furrowed appearance
Keeping all warm and dry
The bats can now call this home

Richard Mackrory

Better Places

There are better trails to walk than this
Better places to drag your skiff
Better places for your shadow to define
Better places to distill the sublime
Better places to fight the foray
Better places for your soul to stray
Better places with a doppler shift
Better places in the cloud and the mist

And at trails end sits the filth and the soot
Littering hedge backs and cracks and nooks
Where the curve of the grass
Meets the splash of the brine
And there the collection of man's filthy shine
Broken boots a rotten chair
Industrial flotsam end of life care

So there are better places not far from here

Better places without joyless tear

Better places to heal your soul

Better places far from this hole

Better places to catch the breeze

Better places to pass with ease

Better places for your mind to stray

Better places for your family to play

Christopher Jelley

Flippant Legacy

My children cannot go barefoot
here amongst the flotsam & jetsam.
A cheap, ill fitting shoe,
bought for a fleeting summer,
now lies sun bleached & brittle.
Permanent
Plastic
Idle

Do you remember the child
who ran down to the sand?
Her memories are golden & linger.

Yet here you taint ours
and make us bitter.

Davina Jelley

Autumn

Autumn

66	The New Fence Offensive	Christopher Jelley
68	Pebble Spots	Davina Jelley
70	Edible Temptress	Christopher Jelley
73	11th October 2014	Tracey Roberts
74	#poetry	Harry Ward
76	Lego Hats	Christopher Jelley
79	To The Point	Will Rayner

The New Fence Offensive

The diesel buzz loads the breeze
Its worrying sounds far beyond the ridge
Carried down on mumbled gasps
The breath of change just over the brow
Past the first fence all barbed and smart
We track along the holloway
Its lazy curves they thread and wind
Meander over centuries long
We walk this way and walk along
And beside it threads the barb top fence
Its staples glimpsed in hedge back gaps
Word pool nodes now fix our rhythm
Changing thoughts to alternate paths
And the diesel hum we had all ignored
Lost in the flow of the drove road cutting

There before us the site laid bare
Its random scoured and sculpted form
Exposing bleak and harvested earth
Unfolds behind the wire some strong
Six track dumpers with dunlop treads
And caterpillar dozers scattered wild
Roaming inside the compound fence
Rutting at their prowling edge
Still in the flow of the drovers' road
The company of fence now guides us down
And behind her curtain the dozers labour
Their scooping buckets feather the earth
With tenderness unexpected
They caress the child in her early hoe
And lay the foundations of her youth

At corner cut she turns back east

And here she spawns defences more

One fence, two fence, three fence, four

One fence

The new fence

Is now the old

For a newer new fence, now stabs at the cold

And as her spines are born into the earth

A temporary fence controls confines

With another beyond below behind

Bigger taller stronger and green

A tighter mesh to frame the machine

At last we cast across the cliff

And hunker down before the bay

Its waves flop and wash away

The diesel hum the sound of the future

Binding fences the suture stitches

Marking land for untold riches

Down here we write upon the rocks

Tiny words for paper tombs

Prepped and printed on electric looms

And the water mumbles her stayed refrain

Again and again

And again and again

Christopher Jelley

Pebble Spots

Rooted and weighted until the next Spring tide,
soft pink, mauve and cardigan grey

Today the wind blows harsh.
Vicious sand flees from the ocean,
cutting close to the land,
blurring the boulder beach.

Head bent,
scarf blown loose,
you relish in the wind.

Look down,
place feet with caution.

The polka dot pebbles in their chalky palette
reveal a second pattern.

Spots bleed with darker hues.
The softness is stolen.
The pebble warmth leeched.
Replaced with dark reflection
and an inner satisfaction.

Davina Jelley

Edible Temptress

Binge the fruit read the labels
Rip at the tide believe the fables
Deeply medicated in our dotage
Death by diagnosis an endless prognosis

Health and youth peeled away
By slithers of time, a feebling foray
We ration our passion
Meaner life in a fashion
Cut our cloth with a simple caution
Binge the fruit, now seven a day
Purge the machine to eradicate decay

The fix-ya elixir, the tonic, the truth
The white coats and surgical, the statistical proof
Mix the mitochondria, borrow the genes
Lab and splice, part lice part machine

Extend repair devolve despair
Distrust disfigure
All new all vigour
Right here right now
New gods new vows
New gown new spleen
No tomb all clean

Keep the faith believe the hype
Count your pills smite the blight
Watch your wrinkles fade away
Secure the medical up-sell today
Know more
Feel less
Ingest the edible temptress

Christopher Jelley

11th October 2014

Visibility, very good
Pressure, rising

We ascend the old way
Following the tracks of the dawn dog-walkers
Picking through a landscape of severed lines

Close cropped billows pinned down
by the ribbon of metal containment
Hedgerows divorced, wondering why
The land each side re-members itself

Mechanical scouring erases ancient settlements
To scraps of stories told by strangers

But we are the strangers
Walking the rift in another's back garden
To the beach and back! (a jolly meander)
Chased home by the clouds to a cosy distance

Back at the rift
They walk
And talk
And watch
And worry
As a giant comes to stay

Tracey Roberts

#poetry

New! Industrial! Credible! Shambles!
Sprung up behind these edible brambles,
Through slow natural growth they pull it,
Constructive power,
The third spent bullet.
Oh these clever words!
Your articulate poet,
Inspired is he by this walk,
But he doesn't want to discuss it,
So now you talk.

Harry Ward

Lego Hats

Lego hats on personnel
High viz vests from Play Mobil
I stretch my hand and play with scale
And marvel at the plant detail
A seven story child is not out of place
Kneeling in the sand with a grin on his face
With toys scattered around his toes
He pushes his diggers and picks at his nose

Tiny hard hats conspire in their threes
In dirt now devoid of grass and trees
Operators connecting from teething years
Manly work all paid in arrears
The diesely dance of steely cutters
Running ditches building shutters
Pushing clay into ditches and flats
With real Tonka toys and Lego hard hats

Hungry machines with citrus tones
Laying foundations for temporary homes
Migrant workers who'll come in waves
Efficiently labouring twenty hour days
Chinese Dutch French connections
With varied skills and diverse affections

Work all hours
Send the money home
Pay for the house
And the life
And the loan

Scrimp and save for a new set of toys
A place with a yard and space for the boys
A corner for a box
To fill with sand
Where toys can sculpt
And re-sculpt this land

Christopher Jelley

NO UNAUTHORISED AC

Site under section

To The Point

This poem remains pinned to here,
With trepidation, angst and fear,
For over there lies nuclear fission,
With rising tides a strange decision.

Sold down the river by the kilowatt hour,
The French and the Chinese supplying our power
It came from high, this nation's loss,
Around our neck an albatross.

The workers they will come in droves,
Block our lanes, arterial roads,
They'll be around for many a year,
For foreign governments to profiteer.

Water water everywhere, no tidal generation?
A legacy of nuclear waste, and social complications,
So much concrete will be poured,
For electricity that we can't afford.

In not too many years from now,
We'll regret not owning this large cash cow,
With many fears and other doubts,
All this to gain a roundabout?

Will Rayner

winter

Winter

85	When Shale Gas Comes to Pass	Christopher Jelley
87	Reach	Matt Bryden
88	Composite One	Various
91	Composite Two	Various
92	Hinkley Point	Geoffrey Bailey
94	Distant Murmers	Lucy Summers
97	The Hypocritical Protestor	Davina Jelley
98	Do You Think	Helga Staddon
100	The Apathetics Have It	Christopher Jelley

When Shale Gas Comes to Pass

The fracking issues
The fracking lies
The fracking deals
The kipper ties
The fracking hunger
The fracking views
The fracking scenes
The fracking news
The fracking science
The fracking choice
The fracking shale gas
The untapped resource
The fracking water
The deep pump tankers
The fracking landscape
The fracking bankers

The fracking decisions
In the name of progress
The fracking pledge
Of CO_2 redress
Is carbon capture
The fracking solution
As emissions hike further
With fracking pollution
The fuel security
Our fracking needs
Our fracking hunger
My fracking heart bleeds
The fracking licence
Now approved by the Queen
We're fracking at your leisure Ma'am
Till shale beds are laid lean

We'll frack the earth
And frack up the walls
And frack ourselves senseless
Waving writs at county halls
We'll frack beneath our bedposts
And frack beneath our stairs
We'll frack our way to hell and back
And frack all woes and cares
And when the oceans swell
And engulf our pleasant land
We'll wonder why our ancestors
Didn't scotch the fracking plans

Christopher Jelley

Reach

Yellow voices from vantages
that oversee construction
reach Mabel and Fable.

Mabel and Fable
tear between them
shreds of a football's orange-stained leather.

Looking down on the tesseracts
of Tetris-regular grey bricks
the wind shears my skin.

My hands burn holding this white card
around which I gather words
like the thinnest strands of wool.

Matt Bryden

Composite One

Two tone mountain and rigger lights
Shock yellow monsters unearthly bites
Casts the winter shadow
All out of kilter
All out of kilter
Between sea and stone

Bat house besieged of robot sentinels
Mangy linkages in landscape strong
Noisy dumpers and diggers throng
This tranquil spot
This tranquil spot
Long shadows long

Berlin wall fencer
Past and present tense the tenser
Heavy waves on square cornered rock
Beauty and the Beast
Beauty and the Beast
Literacy land lock

Composite Two

The squelch of boots and wellies on the rutted track
No gazing out to the vicious sea
The wind makes us turn our backs

To the left unspoilt land bowing in the hurricane
To the right arrogant robots show their disdain

Fickle ivy rustles wildy
We hunker down timely

Grist of Gortex and groat of crow
Hunker from the pressure flow

The resonance of every leaf and every blade
As we shelter low in this grassy glade

The sound describes itself sea ssssh
The sound describes itself sea ssssh

Composite poems by workshop walkers

Hinkley Point

The sea wind shows no mercy here.
It tortures a few twisted trees
and desiccates the hedges,
which outline empty fields.

Remembering its centuries, the drove road
swoops across the valley
in which the giant insects scratch
the earth to make ponds
where strange eggs will be laid.

The fences say 'Keep out' and rectangles
like black biscuits on stalks
eat the light to feed the watching cameras.
The bats are safe in their new house.
Who knows what they may become
when they can feast
on radioactive flies?

Geoffrey Bailey

Distant Murmurs

Scrabbling across mosaic stones,
finding hidden rock pools.
Seaweed popping beneath sand covered boots,
like bubble wrap on birthdays.
Disturbing whelks and sea snails small hands begin to freeze.
What else would you expect from a wintery beach?

Somewhere in the distance,
a murmuring of man-made giants constructing the colossal,
which no amount of tuneful birdsong can drown out.
It punctuates a peaceful scene of waves caressing rock,
with a rumbling like far-off thunder,
threatening to clap.

Lucy Summers

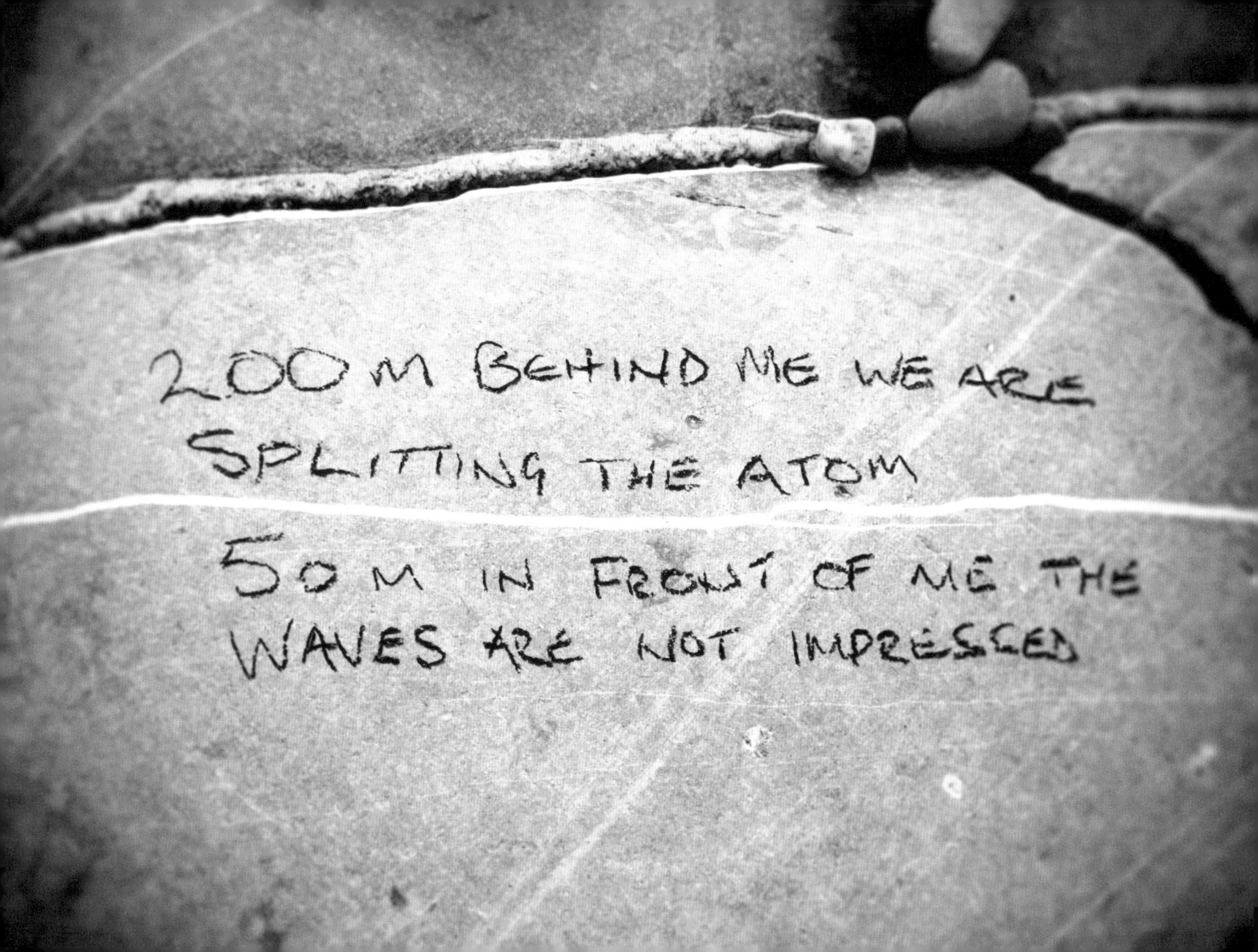
200M BEHIND ME WE ARE
SPLITTING THE ATOM
50M IN FRONT OF ME THE
WAVES ARE NOT IMPRESSED

The Hypocritical Protestor

You considered making the banner
That said no to nuclear power

You'd step out with the march
Shout the rallying chant

Voices heard
Conscience cleared
Homeward bound

Fill the kettle
Fill the bath
Check the mail and Twitter feed
Download images
Spread the word
Connect

I was there
A power to the cause

Reconnect
I was there.

Connections made
Flip the switch and load

Reload
Reconnect
Pause

Connection made

Rethink

Scroll back

Banner unmade

Davina Jelley

Do You Think

Do you think if I
danced the tango, glittering scarf
stamping, stopping
a rhythm of sorts;
they'd watch?

Do you think if I
stripped half naked
frolicking on the
secret sensors
would the camera quiver
and steam up?
They'd notice.

Do you think
I'd entertain
and energize
a sleepy day.

Silent sensors woken up,
Steaming up triggered.

Do you think I'd be watched
Me watching.
You watching.
You watching me watching,
eyes and ears noticing

My moment of fame,
my fifteen minutes,
the world watching,
but I wander on
quiet
acceptance of
them.

Helga Staddon

The Apathetics Have It

Nothing to see?

Nothing to say?

Nothing to add to this trail head today?

No one with an axe to grind?

No one ready to share their mind?

No one with a view to be heard?

No one carrying the canary bird?

Perhaps no one can be bothered to review

And these plans are ripe to run askew!

Is there no one out there carrying the torch

Observe the observers

See the grass become scorched

So where are the poets

The authors

The smiths

Forging opinions

Tagging the shifts

Lacing boots to trace a day

Cutting across these doctrines I portray

Mocking and sacking these words I write

Perhaps it's time you illustrate

My wrong from your right

Go shine that light

Shine that light

Show me what I cannot see

Pen me words from the cultured and free

Your soap box awaits

Your shadow

Your form

Now go fill the board with your loathing and scorn

Or fill it with love and laughter and life

Or fill it with injustice and dogma and strife

Fill it with tears

Fill it with lies

Fill it with mirth

And joy

And slander

Make it murder

Go change its agenda

Box it

Break it

Test it

Fake it

Just don't

Please don't

Leave it sterile

Go post your words

To this three quarter mile

Draw your rapier

Impale your heart

Policies are pinned

Now go take them apart

Go take them apart

Go

Take

Them

Apart

Christopher Jelley

The Final Word

At easy stones throw from this fleeting nest

Deployment skills gather a pace

And plan and plot no skimp no haste

A contraption conceived by the wit of man

Precision of procedure measured to the gram

Whose complexity perplexes the vaster number

The same prepared to waiver the caution

Dismiss the weighting of statistical proportions

To others who have our best needs at heart

(Whose pay deal is likely linked in part)

Now soft-soaping new extensions built

Triple glazed smiles from imported French suits

Will our siblings succour of these tempting fruits

Will it feed the kids

Keep the devils from the door

Provide healthcare wealth-share medication and more?

So who am I to dismiss this cruiser

Our lives entwined with these powers that 'B'

When the wires that grid and supply my juice

Are the same that purge this concrete sluice

The same which chilled and sold us our supper

(Of scallops and fennel and capers and butter)

Now down on the bars

And the stone

And the sand

We gather driftwood and spark our fire

And sink in time with the seaside choir

Of birds and ocean and smokey breeze

And forget the leviathan which slowly rises

Please no mistakes

And no surprises

And dine on elegant ocean fare

Smug in our primal sophistication

A neat example of our indignation

We turn our backs on the futures approaching

Choose to ignore the urbanity encroaching

Walking past this burgeoning blister

With every moment they tighten its bolts

A decade still before the fissile colts

Are leashed and unleashed

Just a stones throw from here

Where we fire up our skillet

On Shurton's tear

Christopher Jelley

Walk the Rift

Step 1   Visit Poetry Pin on your phone

http://poetrypin.info/reveal

Step 2   Travel to the trail head

GPS ref 51.1923 / -3.1462
Ordnance Survey ST202448
Shurton Meadow Gate
TA5 1QQ

Step 3   Follow the poetry pins down to the sea

Step 4   Pick up a pencil and write

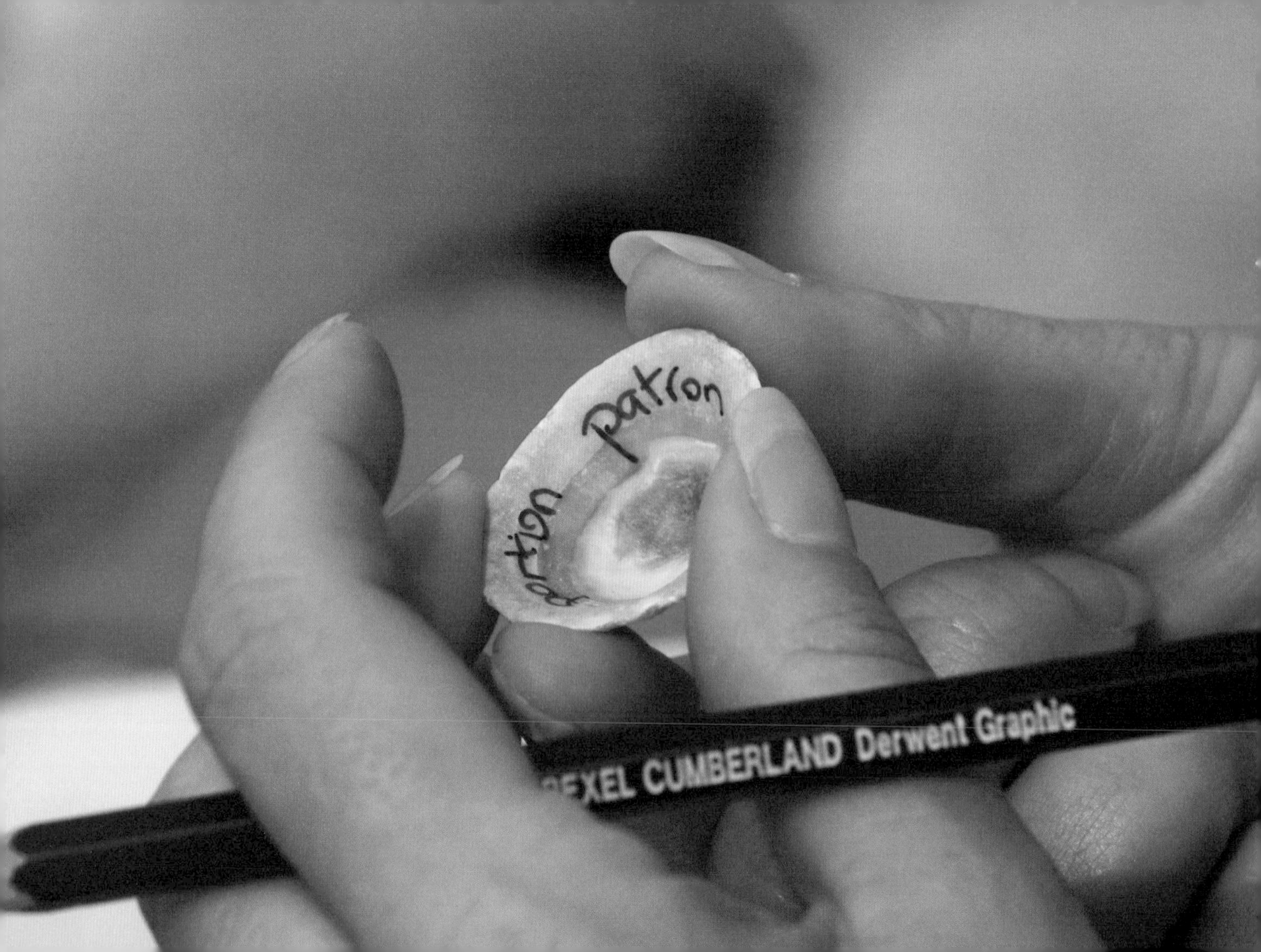
patron
EXEL CUMBERLAND Derwent Graphic

Acknowledgements

The project was funded by EDF Energy as part of the planning agreement with

West Somerset Council for the Hinkley C development

Co-ordinated by ARTlife, The West Somerset Arts Consortium

Poetry Pin was devised and developed by Christopher Jelley

Technical development team Eric Downer and Martin Joiner

Poetry Pin logo designed by Eric Downer

Thank you to all those who came and walked the trail

Credits

All images Davina Jelley

Book copy and layout by Fly Catcher Press

Published by Fly Catcher Press 2015. Copyright © Poetry Pin © Christopher Jelley 2015. Poetry Pin is here by identified as the author of this work in accordance with the Copyrights, Designs and Patents Act 1988. This book is sold subject to the condition that it shall not, by way of trade or otherwise, be lent, resold, hired out, or otherwise circulated without the publisher's prior consent in any form of binding or cover other than that in which it is published. First published in Great Britian 2015 by Fly Catcher Press. www.flycatcherpress.co.uk CIP catalogue record for this book is available from the British Library. ISBN 978-0-9933404-0-6 Printed on FSC ® Printed and bound in Great Britian by Biddles of Kings Lynn.